This is a list of popular acronyms and abbrevi
and chatting.

?	I have a question
?	I don't understand what you mean
?4U	I have a question for you
;S	Gentle warning, like "Hmm? What did you say?"
^^	Meaning "read line" or "read message" above
<3	Meaning "sideways heart" (love, friendship)
<3	Meaning "broken heart"
<33	Meaning "heart or love" (more 3s is a bigger heart)
@TEOTD	At the end of the day
.02	My (or your) two cents worth
1TG, 2TG	Meaning number of items needed for win (online gaming)
1UP	Meaning extra life (online gaming)
121	One-to-one (private chat initiation)
1337	Leet, meaning 'elite'
143	I love you

1432	I love you too
14AA41	One for all, and all for one
182	I hate you
19	Zero hand (online gaming)
10M	Ten man (online gaming)
10X	Thanks
10Q	Thank you
1CE	Once
1DR	I wonder
1NAM	One in a million
2	Meaning "to" in SMS
20	Meaning "location"
2B	To be
2EZ	Too easy
2G2BT	Too good to be true
2M2H	Too much too handle
2MI	Too much information

2MOR   Tomorrow

2MORO Tomorrow

2M2H   Too much to handle

2N8   Tonight

2NTE   Tonight

4   Short for "for" in SMS

411   Meaning "information"

404   I don't know

411   Meaning 'information'

420   Let's get high

420   Meaning "Marijuana"

459   Means I love you (ILY is 459 using keypad numbers)

4AO   For adults only

4COL   For crying out loud

4EAE   Forever and ever

4EVA   Forever

4NR   Foreigner

^5   High-five

511   Too much information (more than 411)

555   Sobbing, crying. (Mandarin Chinese txt msgs)

55555   Crying your eyes out (Mandarin Chinese txt msgs)

55555   Meaning Laughing (In Thai language the number 5 is pronounced 'ha'.)

6Y   Sexy

7K   Sick

81   Meaning Hells Angels (H=8th letter of alphabet, A=1st letter of alphabet)

831   I love you (8 letters, 3 words, 1 meaning)

86   Over

88   Bye-bye (Mandarin Chinese txt msgs)

88   Hugs and kisses

9   Parent is watching

s   Meaning "smile"

w   Meaning "wink"

A3   Anytime, anywhere, any place

AA   Alcoholics Anonymous

AA   As above

AA   Ask about

AAF   As a matter of fact

AAF   As a friend

AAK   Asleep at keyboard

AAK   Alive and kicking

AAMOF As a matter of fact

AAMOI As a matter of interest

AAP   Always a pleasure

AAR   At any rate

AAS   Alive and smiling

AASHTA   As always, Sheldon has the answer (Bike mechanic Sheldon Brown)

AATK   Always at the keyboard

AAYF   As always, your friend

ABBR   Meaning abbreviation

ABC   Already been chewed

ABD   Already been done

ABT   About

ABT2   Meaning 'About to'

ABTA   Meaning Good-bye (signoff)

ABU   All bugged up

AC   Acceptable content

ACC   Anyone can come

ACD   ALT / CONTROL / DELETE

ACDNT   Accident (e-mail, Government)

ACE   Meaning marijuana cigarette

ACK   Acknowledge

ACPT   Accept (e-mail, Government)

ACQSTN   Acquisition (e-mail, Government)

ADAD   Another day, another dollar

ADBB   All done, bye-bye

ADD   Address

ADDY   Address

ADIH   Another day in hell

ADIP   Another day in paradise

ADMIN Administrator

ADMINR   Administrator (Government)

ADN   Any day now

ADR   Address

AE   Area effect (online gaming)

AEAP   As early as possible

AF   April Fools

AF   As *Freak*

AF   Aggression factor (online gaming)

AFC   Away from computer

AFAIAA As far as I am aware

AFAIC   As far as I am concerned

AFAIK   As far as I know

AFAIUI As far as I understand it

AFAP   As far as possible

AFFA   Angels Forever, Forever Angels

AFJ   April Fool's joke

AFK   Away from keyboard

AFZ   Acronym Free Zone

AFPOE   A fresh pair of eyes

AGI   Meaning "agility" (online gaming)

AH   At home

AIAMU   And I am a money's uncle

AIGHT   Alright

AIR   As I remember

AISB   As it should be

AISB   As I said before

AISI   As I see it

AITR   Adult in the room

AKA   Also known as

ALCON   All concerned

ALOL   Actually laughing out loud

AMA   Ask me anything (Reddit)

AMAP   As much as possible

AMBW   All my best wishes

AML   All my love

AMOF   As a matter of fact

A/N   Author's note

AO   Anarchy Online (online gaming)

AOC   Available on cell

AOE   Area of effect (online game)

AOM   Age of majority

AOM   Age of Mythology (online gaming)

AOTA   All of the above

AOYP   Angel on your pillow

APAC   All praise and credit

APP   Application

APP   Appreciate

AQAP   As quick (or quiet) as possible

ARC   Archive (compressed files)

ARE   Acronym rich environment

ARG   Argument

ASIG   And so it goes

ASAP   As soon as possible

A/S/L   Age/sex/location

ASL   Age/sex/location

ASLA   Age/sex/location/availability

AT   At your terminal

ATB   All the best

ATEOTD   At the end of the day

ATM   At the moment

ATSITS All the stars in the sky

ATSL   Along the same line (or lines)

AWC   After awhile crocodile

AWESO Awesome

AWOL   Away without leaving

AWOL   Absent without leave

AYDY   Are you done yet?

AYBABTU   All your base are belong to us (online gaming)

AYEC   At your earliest convenience

AYOR   At your own risk

AYSOS Are you stupid or something?

AYS   Are you serious?

AYT   Are you there?

AYTMTB   And you're telling me this because

AYV   Are you vertical?

AYW   As you were

AYW   As you want / As you wish

AZN   Asian

B	Back
B	Be
B&	Banned
B2B	Business-to-business
B2C	Business-to-consumer
B2W	Back to work
B8	Bait
B9	Boss is watching
B/F	Boyfriend
B/G	Background (personal information request)
B4	Before
B4N	Bye for now
BAG	Busting a gut
BA	Bad *a*
BAE	Before anyone else
BAE	Meaning Babe or baby
BAFO	Best and final offer

BAK   Back at keyboard

BAM   Below average mentality

BAMF   Bad *a* mother *f*

BAO   Be aware of

BAS   Big 'butt' smile

BASIC   Meaning anything mainstream

BASOR   Breathing a sigh of relief

BAU   Business as usual

BAY   Back at ya

BB   Be back

BB   Big brother

BB   Bebi / Baby (Spanish SMS)

BBC   Big bad challenge

BBIAB   Be back in a bit

BBIAF   Be back in a few

BBIAM   Be back in a minute

BBIAS   Be back in a sec

BBL   Be back later

BBN   Bye, bye now

BBQ   Barbeque, "Ownage", shooting score/frag (online gaming)

BBS   Be back soon

BBT   Be back tomorrow

BC   Because

B/C   Because

BC   Be cool

BCNU   Be seeing you

BCOS   Because

BCO   Big crush on

BCOY   Big crush on you

BD   Big deal

BDAY   Birthday

B-DAY   Birthday

BDN   Big darn number

BEG   Big evil grin

BELF   Meaning "Blood Elf" (online gaming)

BF   Boyfriend

BF   Brain fart

BFAW   Best friend at work

BF2   Battlefield 2 (online gaming)

BF   Best friend

BFF   Best friends forever

BFFL   Best friends for life

BFFLNMW   Best friends for life, no matter what

BFD   Big freaking deal

BFG   Big freaking grin

BFFN   Best friend for now

BFN   Bye for now

BG   Big grin

BGWM   Be gentle with me

BHL8   Be home late

BIB   Boss is back

BIBO   Beer in, beer out

BIC   Butt in chair

BIF   Before I forget

BIH   Burn in hell

BIL   Brother in law

BIO   Meaning "I'm going to the bathroom" (or) "Bathroom break"

BION   Believe it or not

BIOYA   Blow it out your *a*

BIOYN   Blow it out your nose

BIS   Best in slot (online gaming)

BISFLATM   Boy, I sure feel like a turquoise monkey!

BITMT   But in the meantime

BL   Belly laugh

BLNT   Better luck next time

Bloke   Meaning Man

BM   Bite me

BME   Based on my experience

BM&Y   Between me and you

BOB   Back off *buddy*

BN   Bad news

BOE   Meaning "bind on equip" (online gaming)

BOHICA Bend over here it comes again

BOL   Best of luck

BOM   *b* of mine

BOLO   Be on the look out

BOOMS Bored out of my skull

BOP   Meaning "bind on pickup" (online gaming)

BOSMKL   Bending over smacking my knee laughing

BOT   Back on topic

BOT   Be on that

BOYF   Boyfriend

BPLM   Big person little mind

BRB   Be right back

BR	Best regards
BRBB	Be right back *b*
BRNC	Be right back, nature calls
BRD	Bored
BRH	Be right here
BRT	Be right there
BSF	But seriously folks
BSOD	Blue screen of death
BSTS	Better safe than sorry
BT	Bite this
BT	Between technologies
BTA	But then again
BTDT	Been there, done that
BTW	By the way
BTYCL	Meaning 'Bootycall'
BUBU	Slang term for the most beautiful of women
BURN	Used to reference an insult

Buff   Meaning "changed and is now stronger" (online gaming)

BWL   Bursting with laughter

BYOB   Bring your own beer

BYOC   Bring your own computer

BYOD   Bring your own device

BYOH   Bat you on (the) head

BYOP   Bring your own paint (paintball)

BYTM   Better you than me

C&G   Chuckle & grin

C4N   Ciao for now

CAD   Control + Alt + Delete

CAD   Short for Canada/Canadian

Cakeday   Meaning Birthday (Reddit)

CAM   Camera (SMS)

CB   Coffee break

CB   Chat break

CB   Crazy *b*

CD9   Code 9, Meaning "parents are around"

CFS   Care for secret?

CFY   Calling for you

CHK   Check

CIAO   Good-bye (Italian word)

CICO   Coffee in, coffee out

CID   Crying in disgrace

CID   Consider it done

CLAB   Crying like a baby

CLD   Could

CLK   Click

CM   Call me

CMAP   Cover my *a* partner (online gaming)

CMB   Call me back

CMGR   Meaning "Community manager"

CMIIW Correct me if I'm wrong

CMON Come on

CNP Continued (in) next post

COB Close of business

COH City of Heroes (online gaming)

COS Because

C/P Cross post

CP Chat post (or continue in IM)

CR8 Create

CRE8 Create

CRA CRA Slang term meaning "crazy"

CRAFT Can't remember a *freaking* thing

CRB Come right back

CRBT Crying really big tears

CRIT Meaning "critical hit" (online gaming)

CRZ Crazy

CRS Can't remember *stuff*

CSG   Chuckle, snicker, grin

CSL   Can't stop laughing

CSS   Counter-Strike Source (online gaming)

CT   Can't talk

CTC   Care to chat?

CTHU   Cracking the *heck* up

CTN   Can't talk now

CTO   Check this out

CU   See you

CU2   See you too

CUA   See you around

CUL   See you later

CULA   See you later alligator

CUL8R   See you later

CUIMD   See you in my dreams

CURLO   See you around like a donut

CWOT   Complete waste of time

CWYL   Chat with you later

CX   Meaning "Correction"

CYA   See you

CYAL8R See you later

CYE   Check your e-mail

CYEP   Close your eyes partner (online gaming)

CYO   See you online

D2   Dedos / fingers (Spanish SMS)

D46?   Down for sex?

DA   Meaning "The"

DAE   Does anyone else?

DAFUQ (What) the *Freak*?

DAM   Don't annoy me

DAoC   Dark Age of Camelot (online gaming)

DBAU   Doing business as usual

DBEYR   Don't believe everything you read

DC   Disconnect

DD   Dear (or Darling) daughter

DD   Due diligence

DDG   Drop dead gorgeous

DEEZ NUTZ   (I think you get what this means)

DEGT   Dear (or Darling) daughter

DERP   Meaning stupid or silly

DF   Don't even go there

DFL   Dead *freaking* last (online gaming)

DGA   Don't go anywhere

DGAF   Don't give a *freak*

DGT   Don't go there

DGTG   Don't go there, girlfriend

DGYF   Dang, girl you fine

DH   Dear (or Darling) husband

DHU   Dinosaur hugs (used to show support)

DIIK   Darned if I know

DIKU   Do I know you?

DILLIGAF   Do I look like I give a *freak*?

DILLIGAS   Do I look like I give a sugar?

DIS   Did I say?

DITYID Did I tell you I'm distressed?

DIY   Do it yourself

DKDC   Don't know, don't care

DKP   Dragon kill points (online gaming)

D/L   Download

DL   Download

DL   Down low

DL   Dead link

DLBBB   Don't let (the) bed bugs bite

DLTBBB Don't let the bed bugs bite

DM   Doesn't matter

DM   Direct message (Twitter slang)

DM	Do me
DM	Dungeon Master (online gaming)
DMNO	Dude Man No Offense
DMY	Don't mess yourself
DN	Down
DNC	Does not compute (meaning I do not understand)
DNR	Dinner (SMS)
DNT	Don't
d00d	Dude
DOE	Daughter of Eve
DORBS	Meaning "Adorable"
DOT	Damage over time (online gaming)
Downvote	Voting negatively on a thread
DPS	Damage per second (online gaming)
DQMOT	Don't quote me on this
DR	Didn't read
DS	Dear (or Darling) son

DTR   Define the relationship

DTRT   Do the right thing

DTS   Don't think so

DTTD   Don't touch that dial

DUPE   Duplicate

DUR   Do you remember?

DV8   Deviate

DW   Dear (or Darling) wife

DWF   Divorced white female

DWM   Divorced white male

DXNRY   Dictionary

DYNWUTB   Do you know what you are talking about?

DYFI   Did you find it?

DYFM   Dude, you fascinate me

DYJHIW Don't you just hate it when...?

DYOR   Do your own research (common stock market chat slang)

E   Ecstasy

E   Enemy (online gaming)

E1   Everyone

E123 Easy as one, two, three

E2EG Ear to ear grin

EAK   Eating at keyboard

EBKAC Error between keyboard and chair

ED   Erase display

EF4T Effort

EG   Evil grin

EI   Eat it

EIP   Editing in progress

ELI5   Explain like I'm 5

EM   E-mail (Twitter slang)

EMA   E-mail address (Twitter slang)

EMBAR Meaning "Embarassing"

EMFBI Excuse me for butting in

EMFBI Excuse me for jumping in

EMSG E-mail message

ENUF Enough

EOD End of day

EOD End of discussion

EOL End of lecture

EOL End of life

EOM End of message

EOM End of month

EOS End of show

EOT End of transmission

EOY End of year

EQ EverQuest (online gaming)

ERP Meaning "Erotic Role-Play" (online gaming)

ERS2 Eres tz / are you (Spanish SMS)

ES Erase screen

ESAD Eat *S* and die!

ETA   Estimated time (of) arrival

ETA   Edited to add

EVA   Ever

EVO   Evolution

EWG   Evil wicked grin (in fun, teasing)

EWI   Emailing while intoxicated

EXTRA   Meaning over the top

EYC   Excitable, yet calm

EZ   Easy

EZY   Easy

F   Meaning female

F2F   Face to face

F2P   Free to play (online gaming)

FAAK   Falling asleep at keyboard

FAB   Fabulous

Facepalm   Used to represent the gesture of "smacking your forehead with your palm" to express embarrassment or frustration

FAF   Funny as *freak*

FAQ   Frequently asked questions

FAY   *Freak* all you

FB   Facebook

FBB   Meaning "Facebook buddy"

FBC   Facebook chat

FBF   Flashback Friday

FBF   Meaning "Facebook friend"

FBF   Fat boy food (e.g. pizza, burgers, fries)

FBFR   FaceBook friend

FBM   Fine by me

FBO   Facebook official (An official update from Facebook)

FBOW   For better or worse

FC   Fingers crossed

FC   Full card (online gaming)

FC'INGO   For crying out loud

FCOL   For crying out loud

Feelsbadman   A social meme that means to feel negative.

Feelsbatman   A social meme taking "feelsbadman" to the extreme. This references the DC super hero Batmanbecause he witnessed the murder of his parents.

Feelsgoodman   A social meme that means to feel positive.

FEITCTAJ   *Freak* 'em if they can't take a joke

FF   Follow Friday (Twitter slang)

FFA   Free for all (online gaming)

FFS   For *freak'*sakes

FICCL   Frankly I couldn't care a less

FIF   *Freak* I'm funny

FIIK   *Freaked* if I know

FIIOOH Forget it, I'm out of here

FIL   Father in law

FIMH   Forever in my heart

FISH   First in, still here

FITB	Fill in the blank
FML	*Freak* My Life
FOMC	Falling off my chair
FOAD	*Freak* off and die
FOAF	Friend of a friend
FOMCL	Falling off my chair laughing
FRT	For real though
FTBOMH	From the bottom of my heart
FTFY	Fixed that for you
FTL	For the loss
FTW	For the win
FU	*Freak* you
FUBAR	Fouled up beyond all recognition
FUBB	Fouled up beyond belief
FUD	Face up deal (online gaming)
FUTAB	Feet up, take a break
FW	Forward

FWB   Friend with benefits

FWIW   For what it's worth

FWM   Fine with me

FWP   First world problems

FYEO   For your eyes only

FYA   For your amusement

FYIFor your information

G   Grin

G   Giggle

G+   Google+

G/F   Girlfriend

G2CU   Good to see you

G2G   Got to go

G2GICYAL8ER   Got to go I'll see you later

G2R   Got to run

G2TU	Got to tell you
G4C	Going for coffee
G9	Genius
GA	Go ahead
GAC	Get a clue
GAFC	Get a *freaking* clue
GAL	Get a life
GANK	Meaning a player ambush or unfair player kill (online gaming)
GAS	Got a second?
GAS	Greetings and salutations
GB	Goodbye
GBTW	Get back to work
GBU	God bless you
GD	Good
GDR	Grinning, ducking, and running
GD/R	Grinning, ducking, and running
GFI	Go for it

GF   Girl friend

GFN   Gone for now

GG   Gotta Go

GG   Good Game (online gaming)

GG   Brother (Mandarin Chinese txt msgs)

GGA   Good game, all (online gaming)

GGE1   Good game, everyone (online gaming)

GGU2   Good game, you too

GGMSOT   Gotta get me some of that

GGOH   Gotta Get Outa Here

GGP   Got to go pee

GH   Good hand (online gaming)

GIAR   Give it a rest

GIC   Gift in crib (online gaming)

GIGO   Garbage in, garbage out

GIRL   Guy in real life

GJ   Good job

GL   Good luck

GL2U   Good luck to you (online gaming)

GLA   Good luck all (online gaming)

GL/HF   Good luck, have fun (online gaming)

GLE   Good luck everyone (online gaming)

GLE1   Good luck everyone (online gaming)

GLNG   Good luck next game (online gaming)

GMBA   Giggling my butt off

GMTA   Great minds think alike

GMV   Got my vote

GN   Good night

GNA   Good night all

GNE1   Good night everyone

GNIGHTGood night

GNITE   Good night

GNSD   Good night, sweet dreams

GOAT   Greatest of all Time(s)

GOI   Get over it

GOL   Giggling out loud

GOMB Get off my back

GPOY   Gratuitous picture of yourself

GR8   Great

GRATZ Congratulations

GRL   Girl

GRWG Get right with God

GR&D   Grinning, running and ducking

GS   Good shot

GS   Good split (online gaming)

GT   Good try

GTFO   Get the *freak* out

GTFOH Get the *freak* outta here

GTG   Got to go

GTM   Giggling to myself

GTRM   Going to read mail

GTSY   Great (or good) to see you

GUCCI Good

GUD   Good

GWHTLC   Glad we had this little chat

H   Hug

H8   Hate

H8TTU Hate to be you

HAG1   Have a good one

HAK   Hug and kiss

HALP   Help (Discord)

HAU   How about you?

H&K   Hugs & kisses

H2CUS   Hope to see you soon

HAGN   Have a good night

HAGO   Have a good one

HAND   Have a nice day

HAWT   Have a wonderful day (out-dated, see next in list)

HAWT   Meaning "sexy" or "attractive"

HB   Hurry back

HB   Hug back

HBD   Happy birthday

H-BDAY Happy Birthday

HBU   How about you?

HF   Have fun

HFAC   Holy flipping animal crackers

H-FDAY Happy Father's Day

HHIS   Head hanging in shame

HIFW   How I felt when... (Used with photo or gif)

HL   Half Life (online gaming)

HLA   Hola / hello (Spanish SMS)

H-MDAY   Happy Mother's Day

HMU   Hit me up

HNL   (w)Hole 'nother level

HOAS   Hold on a second

HP   Hit points / Health points (online gaming)

HRU   How are you?

HTH   Hope this helps

HUB   Head up butt

HUYA   Head up your *butt*

HV   Have

HVH   Heroic Violet Hold (online gaming)

HW   Homework

HYFR   Hell yeah, *Freaking* right!

I2   I too (me too)

IA8   I already ate

IAAA   I am an accountant

IAAD   I am a doctor

IAAL   I am a lawyer

IAC   In any case

IAE   In any event

IANAC   I am not a crook

IANAL   I am not a lawyer

IAO   I am out (of here)

IB   I'm back

IB   I'm back

IC   I see

ICAM   I couldn't agree more

ICBW   It could be worse

ICEDI   I can't even discuss it

ICFILWU   I could fall in love with you

ICYMI   In case you missed it (Twitter slang)

IDBI   I don't believe it

IDC   I don't care

IDGAF   I don't give a *freak*

IDK	I don't know
IDTS	I don't think so
IDUNNO	I don't know
IFYP	I feel your pain
IG	Instagram
IG2R	I got to run
IGHT	I got high tonight
IGN	I (I've) got nothing
IGP	I got to (go) pee
IHNI	I have no idea
IIRC	If I remember correctly
IIIO	Intel inside, idiot outside
IK	I know
IKR	I know, right?
ILBL8	I'll be late
ILU	I love you
ILUM	I love you man

ILYSM   I love you so much

ILY   I love you

IM   Instant message

IMAO   In my arrogant opinion

IMHO   In my humble opinion

ImL   (in Arial font) Means I love you (a way of using the American sign language in text)

IMNSHO   In my not so humble opinion

IMO   In my opinion

IMS   I am sorry

IMSB   I am so bored

IMTM   I am the man

IMU   I miss you

INAL   I'm not a lawyer

INC   Meaning "incoming" (online gaming)

INV   Meaning "Invite"

IOMH   In over my head

IOW   In other words

IRL   In real life

IRMC   I rest my case

ISLY   I still love you

ISO   In search of

ITAM   It's The Accounting, Man (financial blogs)

ITT   In This Thread

ITYK   I thought you knew

IUSS   If you say so

IWALU I will always love you

IWAWO I want a way out

IWIAM Idiot wrapped in a moron

IWSN   I want sex now

IYKWIM If you know what I mean

IYO   In your opinion

IYQ   Meaning "I like you"

IYSS   If you say so

j00	You
j00r	Your
JAC	Just a second
JAM	Just a minute
JAS	Just a second
JC (J/C)	Just checking
JDI	Just do it
JELLY	Meaning "jealous"
JFF	Just for fun
JFGI	Just *freaking* Google it
JIC	Just in case
JJ (J/J)	Just joking
JJA	Just joking around
JK (J/K)	Just kidding
JLMK	Just let me know
JMO	Just my opinion
JP	Just playing

JP   Jackpot (online gaming, bingo games)

JT (J/T) Just teasing

JTLYK   Just to let you know

JV   Joint venture

JW   Just wondering

K   Okay

KK   Knock, knock

KK   Okay, Okay!

K8T   Katie

k/b   Keyboard

KB   Keyboard

KB   Kick butt (online gaming)

KDFU   Means Cracking (K) the (D as in Da) *freak* up

KEWL   Cool

KEYA   I will key you later

KEYME   Key me when you get in

KFY   Kiss for you

KIA   Know it all

KISS   Keep it simple, stupid

KIT   Keep in touch

KMA   Kiss my *a*

KMK   Kiss my keister

KMT   Kiss my tushie

KOC   Kiss on cheek

KOS   Kid over shoulder

KOS   Kill on sight

KOW   Knock on wood

KOTC   Kiss on the cheek

KOTL   Kiss on the lips

KNIM   Know what I mean?

KNOW   Meaning "knowledge"

KPC   Keeping parents clueless

KS   Kill then steal (online gaming)

KSC   Kind (of) sort (of) chuckle

KT   Katie

KUTGW Keep up the good work

L2G   Like to go?

L2G   (would) Love to go

L2K   Like to come

L2P   Learn to play

l33t   Leet, meaning 'elite'

L8R   Later

L8RG8R Later, gator

LBAY   Laughing back at you

LBS   Laughing, but serious

LBVS   Laughing, but very serious

LD   Later, dude

LD   Long distance

LDO   Like, duh obviously

LEMENO   Let me know

LERK   Leaving easy reach of keyboard

LFD   Left for day

LFG   Looking for group (online gaming)

LFG   Looking for guard (online gaming)

LFM   Looking for more (online gaming)

LGH   Let's get high

LH6   Let's have sex

LHSX   Let's have sex

LHM   Lord help me

LHO   Laughing head off

LI   LinkedIn

LIC   Like I care

LIK   Meaning liquor

LIMT   Laugh in my tummy

LIT   Meaning really good or something fun and exciting

LLGB   Love, later, God bless

LLS   Laughing like *silly*

LMAO   Laughing my *a* off

LMBO   Laughing my butt off

LMFAO Laughing my freaking *a* off

LMIRL   Let's meet in real life

LMK   Let me know

LMMFAO   Laughing my mother freaking a** off

LMNK   Leave my name out

LMS   Like my status (Facebook)

LNT   Meaning lost in translation

LOA   List of acronyms

LOL   Laughing out loud

LOL   Laugh out loud

LOL   Lots of love

LOLH   Laughing out loud hysterically

LOLO   Lots of love

LOLWTF   Laughing out loud (saying) "What the *freak*?"

LOTI   Laughing on the inside

LOTR   Lord of The Rings (online gaming)

LQTM   Laughing quietly to myself

LSHMBH   Laugh so hard my belly hurts

LSV   Language, sex and violence

LTD   Living the dream

LTLWDLS   Let's twist like we did last summer

LTNS   Long time no see

LTOD   Laptop of death

LTS   Laughing to self

LULT   Love you long time

LULZ   Meaning joke, or for laughs

LVM   Left voice mail

LWOS   Laughing without smiling

LY   Love ya

LYLAS   Love you like a sis

LYLC   Love you like crazy

LYSM   Love you so much

M$ Microsoft

M8   Mate

MB   Mamma's boy

MBS   Mom behind shoulder

MC   Merry Christmas

MDIAC   My Dad is a cop

MEGO   My eyes glaze over

MEH   Meaning a "shrug" or shrugging shoulders

MEH   Meaning a "so-so" or "just okay"

MEHH   Meaning a "sigh" or sighing

MEZ   Meaning "mesmerize" (online gaming)

MFI   Mad for it

MFW   My face when... (Used with photo or gif)

MGB   May God bless

MGMT   Management

MHOTY My hat (is) off to you

MIRL   Me in real life

MIRL   Meet in real life

MISS.(number) Meaning "child and her age". Miss.3 would be a 3-year old daughter

MKAY   Meaning "Mmm, okay"

MLM   Meaning give the middle finger

MM   Sister (Mandarin Chinese txt msg)

MMK   Meaning okay? (as a question)

MNC   Mother nature calls

MNSG   Mensaje (message in Spanish)

MOD   Moderator

MOD   Modification (online gaming)

MORF   Male or female?

MOMBOY   Mamma's boy

MOO   My own opinion

MOOS   Member of the opposite sex

MOS   Mother over shoulder

MOSS   Member of same sex

MP   Mana points (online gaming)

MR.(number)   Meaning "child and his age". Mr.3 would be a 3-year old son

MRT   Modified ReTweet (Twitter slang)

MRW   My reaction when... (Used with photo or gif)

MSG   Message

MTF   More to follow

MTFBWU   May the force be with you

MU   Miss U (you)

MUAH   Multiple unsuccessful attempts (at/to) humor

MUSM   Miss you so much

MWAH   Meaning "kiss" (it is is the sound made when kissing through the air)

MYO   Mind your own (business)

MYOB   Mind your own business

n00b   Newbie

N1   Nice one

N2M   Nothing too much

NADT   Not a darn thing

NALOPKT   Not a lot of people know that

NANA   Not now, no need

NBD   No big deal

NBFAB No bad for a beginner (online gaming)

NC   Nice crib (online gaming)

ND   Nice double (online gaming)

NE   Any

NE1   Anyone

NERF   Meaning "Changed and is now weaker" (online gaming)

NFM   None for me / Not for me

NFM	Not for me
NGL	Not gonna (going to) lie
NFS	Need for Speed (online gaming)
NFS	Not for sale
NFW	No *freaking* way
NFW	Not for work
NFWS	Not for work safe
NH	Nice hand (online gaming)
NIFOC	Naked in front of computer
NIGI	Now I get it
NIMBY	Not in my back yard
NIROK	Not in reach of keyboard
NLT	No later than
NM	Nothing much
NM	Never mind
NM	Nice meld (online gaming)
NMH	Not much here

NMJC   Nothing much, just chilling

NMU   Not much, you?

NO1   No one

NOOB   Meaning someone who is bad at (online) games

NOWL   Meaning "knowledge"

NOYB   None of your business

NP   No problem

NPC   Non-playing character (online gaming)

NQT   Newly qualified teacher

NR   Nice roll (online gaming)

NRN   No response/reply necessary

NS   Nice score (online gaming)

NS   Nice split (online gaming)

NSA   No strings attached

NSFL   Not safe for life

NSFW   Not safe for work

NSISR   Not sure if spelled right

NT   Nice try

NTHING   Nothing (SMS)

NTS   Note to self

NVM   Never mind

NVR   Never

NW   No way

NOW   No way out

O4U   Only for you

O   Opponent (online gaming)

O   Meaning "hugs"

O   Over

OA   Online auctions (see more auction abbreviations)

OATUS   On a totally unrelated subject

OB   Oh baby

OB   Oh brother

OBV   Obviously

OFC   Of course

OG   Original gangster

OGIM   Oh God, it's Monday

OH   Overheard

OHHEMMGEE   Meaning "Oh My God" (alternate of OMG)

OI   Operator indisposed

OIB   Oh, I'm back

OIC   Oh, I see

OJ   Only joking

OL   Old lady

OLL   Online love

OM   Old man

OM   Oh, my

OMAA   Oh, my aching *A* (butt)

OMDB   Over my dead body

OMFG   Oh my *freaking* God

omfglmaobbqrofl
copteriss   oh my *freaking* god, laugh my *a* off,
owned, roll on floor spinning around I'm so sad

OMG   Oh my God

OMG   Oh my gosh

OMGYG2BK   Oh my God, you got to be kidding

OMGYS Oh my gosh you suck

OMS   On my soul (meaning "promise")

OMW   On my way

ONL   Online

OO   Over and out

OOC   Out of character

OOH   Out of here

OOTD   One of these days

OOTO   Out of the office

OP   On phone

ORLY   Oh really?

OS   Operating system

OT   Off topic (discussion forums)

OTB   Off to bed

OTFL   On the floor laughing

OTL   Out to lunch

OTOH   On the other hand

OTP   On the phone

OTT   Over the top

OTTOMH   Off the top of my head

OTW   Off to work

OVA   Over

OYO   On your own

P   Partner (online gaming)

P2P   Parent to parent

P2P   Peer to peer

P2P   Pay to play (online gaming)

P911 Parents coming into room alert

PAT Meaning "patrol" (online gaming)

PAW Parents are watching

PBOOK Phonebook (e-mail)

PC Player character (online gaming)

PCM Please call me

PDA Personal display (of) affection

PDH Pretty darn happy

PDS Please don't shoot

PDQ Pretty darn quick

PEEPS People

PFT Pretty *freaking* tight

PIC Picture

PIP Peeing in pants (laughing hard)

PIR Parents in room

PISS Put in some sugar

PITA Pain in the *butt*

PKMN   Pokemon (online gaming)

PL8   Plate

PLD   Played

PLMK   Please let me know

PLS   Please

PLU   People like us

PLZ   Please

PLZTLME   Please tell me

PM   Private Message

PMFI   Pardon me for interrupting

PMFJI   Pardon me for jumping in

PMSL   Pee myself laughing

POAHF   Put on a happy face

POIDH   Picture, or it didn't happen

PORN   Meaning pornography

POS   Parent over shoulder

POT   Meaning "potion" (online gaming)

POV   Point of view

POV   Privately owned vehicle

PPL   People

PPU   Pending pick-up

PRESH   Precious

PROBS   Probably

PROLLY   Probably

PROGGY   Meaning computer program

PRT   Party

PRT   Please Retweet (Twitter slang)

PRW   People/parents are watching

PSOS   Parent standing over shoulder

PSP   Playstation Portable

PST   Please send tell (online gaming)

PTFO   Pass the *freak* out

PTIYPASI   Put that in your pipe and smoke it

PTL   Praise the Lord

PTMM Please tell me more

PTO Paid time off

PTO Personal time off

PTO Parent Teacher Organization

PUG Pick up group (online gaming)

PVE Player vs enemy, Player versus environment (online gaming)

PVP Player versus player (online gaming)

PWN Meaning "own"

PXT Please explain that

PU That stinks!

PUKS Pick up kids (SMS)

PYT Pretty young thing

PZ Peace

PZA Pizza

Q   Queue

Q4U   (I have a) question for you

QC   Quality control

QFE   Question for everyone

QFI   Quoted for idiocy

QFI   Quoted for irony

QFT   Quoted for truth

QIK   Quick

QL   Quit laughing

QOTD   Quote of the day

QQ (qq) (Q_Q)   Meaning "crying eyes"

QQ   Quick question

QSL   Reply

QSO   Conversation

QT   Cutie

QTPI   Cutie pie

R Meaning "are"

R8 Rate (SMS)

RBAY Right back at you

RFN Right *freaking* now

RGR Roger (I agree, I understand)

RHIP Rank has its privileges

RIP Rest in peace

RL Real life

RLY Really

RME Rolling my eyes

RMLB Read my lips baby

RMMM Read my mail, man

ROFL Rolling on floor laughing

ROFLCOPTER Rolling on floor laughing and spinning around

ROFLMAO Rolling on the floor, laughing my *butt* off

ROTFL Rolling on the floor laughing

ROTFLUTS Rolling on the floor laughing unable to speak

RS   Runescape (online gaming)

RSN   Real soon now

RT   Roger that

RT   Retweet (Twitter slang)

RTBS   Reason to be single

RTFM   Read the *freaking* manual

RTFQ   Read the *freaking* question

RTHX   Meaning "Thanks for the RT (Retweet)" (Twitter slang)

RTMS   Read the manual, stupid

RTNTN   Retention (email, Government)

RTRCTV Retroactive (email, Government)

RTRMT   Retirement (email, Government)

RTSM   Read the stupid manual

RTWFQ   Read the whole *freaking* question

RU   Are you?

RUMOF   Are you male or female?

RUT   Are u (you) there?

RUOK   Are you okay?

RX   Regards

RW   Real world

RX   Meaning drugs or prescriptions

RYB   Read your Bible

RYO   Roll your own

RYS   Read your screen

RYS   Are you single?

S2R   Send to receive (meaning send me your picture to get mine)

S2S   Sorry to say

S4L   Spam for life

SAL   Such a laugh

SAT   Sorry about that

SAVAGE   Slang for a shockingly careless expression or response to an event or message

SB   Should be

SB   Smiling back

SBIA   Meaning Standing back in amazement

SBT   Sorry 'bout that

SC   Stay cool

SD   Sweet dreams

SDMB   Sweet dreams, my baby

SENPAI   Meaning someone older than you, someone you look up to

SEO   Search engine optimization

SETE   Smiling Ear-to-Ear

SELFIE   A photo that's taken of oneself for social media sharing

SFAIK   So far as I know

SH   Same here

SH^   Shut up

SHID   Slapping head in disgust

SHIP   Slang for "wishing two people were in a relationship"

SICNR   Sorry, I could not resist

SIG2R   Sorry, I got to run

SIHTH   Stupidity is hard to take

SIMYC   Sorry I missed your call

SIR   Strike it rich

SIS   Snickering in silence

SIS   Meaning sister

SIT   Stay in touch

SITD   Still in the dark

SJW   Social justice warrior

SK8   Skate

SK8NG   Skating

SK8R   Skater

SK8RBOI   Skater Boy

SLAP   Sounds like a plan

SM   Social media

SMAZED   Smoky haze (marijuana stoned)

SMEXI Combination of sexy and Mexican, used to describe attractive people

SMH   Shaking my head

SMHID Scratching my head in disbelief

SNAFU Situation normal all fouled up

SNERT Snot nosed egotistical rude teenager

SO   Significant other

SOAB   Son of a *B*

S'OK   Meaning It' (s) okay (ok)

SOL   Sooner or later

SOMY   Sick of me yet?

SorG   Straight or Gay?

SOS   Meaning help

SOS   Son of Sam

SOT   Short of time

SOTMG Short of time, must go

SOWM Someone with me

SPK   Speak (SMS)

SRSLY	Seriously
SPST	Same place, same time
SPTO	Spoke to
SQ	Square
SRY	Sorry
SS	So sorry
SSDD	Same stuff, different day
SSIF	So stupid it's funny
SSINF	So stupid it's not funny
ST&D	Stop texting and drive
STFU	Shut the *freak* up
STR8	Straight
STW	Search the Web
SU	Shut up
SUITM	See you in the morning
SUL	See you later
SUP	What's up?

SUTH   So use(d) to haters (Facebook)

SUX   Meanings sucks or "it sucks"

SUYF   Shut up you fool

SWAG   Meaning free stuff and giveaways from tech tradeshows (definition)

SWAG   Scientific wild *a* guess

SWAK   Sent (or sealed) with a kiss

SWALK   Sealed (or sealed) with a loving kiss

SWAT   Scientific wild *butt* guess

SWL   Screaming with laughter

SWMBO   She who must be obeyed. Meaning wife or partner

SYL   See you later

SYS   See you soon

SYY   Shut your yapper

T+   Think positive

T4BU   Thanks for being you

T:)T   Think happy thoughts

TA   Thanks a lot

TAFN   That's all for now

TAM   Tomorrow a.m.

TANK   Meaning really strong

TANKED   Meaning "owned"

TANKING   Meaning "owning"

TARFU   Things Are Really *fouled* Up.

TAU   Thinking about u (you)

TAUMUALU   Thinking about you miss you always love you

TBAG   Process of disgracing a corpse, taunting a fragged/killed player (online gaming)

TBC   To be continued

TBD   To be determined

TBH   To be honest

TBL   Text back later

TBT   Throwback Thursday (Twitter slang)

TC   Take care

TCB   Take care of business

TCOY   Take care of yourself

TD   Tower defense (online gaming)

TD2M   Talk dirty to me

TDTM   Talk dirty to me

TFF   Too *freaking* funny

TFS   Thanks for sharing

TFTF   Thanks for the follow (Twitter slang)

TFTI   Thanks for the invitation

TFTT   Thanks for this tweet (Twitter slang)

TG   Thank goodness

TGIF   Thank God it's Friday

THNQ   Thank-you (SMS)

THNX   Thanks

THOT   That wh*re over there

THT	Think happy thoughts
THX	Thanks
TIA	Thanks in advance
TIAD	Tomorrow is another day
TIC	Tongue-in-cheek
TIL	Today I learned
TILIS	Tell it like it is
TIR	Teacher in room
TLK2UL8R	Talk to you later
TL	Too long
TL;DR	Too long; didn't read
TM	Trust me
TMA	Take my advice
TMB	Text me back
TMB	Tweet me back (Twitter slang)
TMI	Too much information
TMOT	Trust me on this

TMTH   Too much to handle

TMYL   Tell me your location

TMWFI Take my word for it

TNSTAAFL   There's no such thing as a free lunch

TNT   Til next time

TOJ   Tears of joy

TOS   Terms of service

TOTES   Totally

TOU   Thinking of you

TOY   Thinking of you

TPM   Tomorrow p.m.

TPTB   The powers that be

TQ   Te quiero / I love you (Spanish SMS)

TSH   Tripping so hard

TSNF   That's so not fair

TSTB   The sooner, the better

TT   Trending topic (Twitter slang)

TTFN	Ta ta for now
TTLY	Totally
TTTT	These things take time
TTUL	Talk to you later
TU	Thank you
TUI	Turning you in
TURNT	Meaning excitement, turned up
TWSS	That's what she said
TTG	Time to go
TTYAFN	Talk to you awhile from now
TTYL	Talk to you later
TTYS	Talk to you soon
TY	Thank you
TYFC	Thank you for charity (online gaming)
TYFYC	Thank you for your comment
TYS	Told you so
TYT	Take your time

TYSO   Thank you so much

TYAFY   Thank you and *freak* you

TYVM   Thank you very much

TX   Thanks

^URS   Up yours

UCMU   You crack me up

UDI   Unidentified drinking injury

UDM   U (You) da (the) man

UDS   Ugly domestic scene

UFB   Un *freaking* believable

UFN   Until further notice

UFWM   You *freaking* with me?

UGTBK   You've got to be kidding

UHGTBSM   You have got to be s#$t*ing me!

UKTR   You know that's right

UL   Upload

U-L   Meaning "You will"

UNA   Use no acronyms

UN4TUN8   Unfortunate

UNBLEFBLE   Unbelievable

UNCRTN   Uncertain

UNPC   Un- (not) politically correct

UOK   (Are) You ok?

UR   You are / You're

UR2YS4ME   You are too wise for me

URA*   You are a star

URH   You are hot

URSKTM   You are so kind to me

URTM   You are the man

URW   You are welcome

USBCA   Until something better comes along

USU	Usually
UT	Unreal Tournament (online gaming)
UT2L	You take too long
UTM	You tell me
UV	Unpleasant visual
UW	You're welcome
UX	User experience

V	Very
VAT	Value added tax
VBL	Visible bra line
VBS	Very big smile
VC	Voice chat
VEG	Very evil grin
VFF	Very freaking funny
VFM	Value for money

VGC   Very good condition

VGG   Very good game (online gaming)

VGH   Very good hand (online gaming)

VIP   Very important person

VM   Voice mail

VN   Very nice

VNH   Very nice hand (online gaming)

VoIP   Voice over Internet Protocol (definition)

VRY   Very

VSC   Very soft chuckle

VSF   Very sad face

VWD   Very well done (online gaming)

VWP   Very well played (online gaming)

W@   What?

W/   With

W/B   Welcome back

W3   WWW (Web address)

W8   Wait

WAH   Working at home

WAJ   What a jerk

WAM   Wait a minute

WAN2   Want to? (SMS)

WAN2TLK   Want to talk

WAREZ Meaning pirated (illegally gained) software

WAS   Wait a second

WAS   Wild *a* guess

WAT   What

WAWA Where are we at?

WAYF   Where are you from?

W/B   Write back

WB   Welcome back

WBS   Write back soon

WBU   What about you?

WC   Welcome

WC   Who cares

WCA   Who cares anyway

W/E   Whatever

W/END Weekend

WE   Whatever

WEBO   Webopedia

WEEBO Describes a person obsessed with of Japanese culture

WEP   Weapon (online gaming)

WH5   Who, what, when, where, why

WHATEVES   Whatever

WIBNI Wouldn't it be nice if

WDALYIC   Who died and left you in charge

WDYK   What do you know?

WDYT   What do you think?

WGACA What do you think?

WIIFM   What's in it for me?

WISP   Winning is so pleasurable

WITP   What is the point?

WITW   What in the world

WIU   Wrap it up

WK   Week

WKD   Weekend

WRT   With regard to

WL   Whatta loser

W/O   Without

WOA   Work of Art

WOKE   Slang for people who are aware of current social issues, and politics

WOMBAT   Waste of money, brains and time

WOW   World of Warcraft (online gaming)

WRK   Work

WRU   Where are you?

WRU@ Where are you at?

WRUD   What are you doing?

WTB   Want to buy (online gaming)

WTF   What the *freak* ?

WTFE   What the *freak* ever

WTFO   What the *freak* ?, over.

WTG   Way to go

WTGP   Want to go private (talk out of public chat area)

WTH   What the heck?

WTM   Who's the man?

WTS   Want to sell? (online gaming)

WTT   Want to trade? (online gaming)

WU   What's up?

WUCIWUG   What you see is what you get

WUF   Where are you from?

WUP   What's up?

WUT   Meaning "what"

WUW   What u (you) want?

WUU2   What are you up to?

WUZ   Meaning "was"

WWJD   What would Jesus do?

WWNC   Will wonders never cease

WWYC   Write when you can

WYCM   Will you call me?

WYD   What (are) you doing?

WYGAM   When you get a minute

WYHAM   When you have a minute

WYLEI   When you least expect it

WYSIWYG   What you see is what you get

WYWH   Wish you were here

X-1-10   Meaning "Exciting"

X   Kiss

X!   Meaning "a typical woman"

XD   Meaning "really hard laugh" (where D is a smiley mouth)

XD   Meaning a "devilish smile"

XME   Excuse Me

XOXOXO   Hugs & Kisses

XLNT   Excellent

XLR8   Meaning "faster" or "going faster"

XPOST   Meaning Cross-post. A link posted to a subreddit that was already shared on a different subreddit (Reddit)

XYL   Ex-young lady, meaning wife. (amateur radio)

XYZ   Examine your zipper

Y?   Why?

Y   Meaning Yawn

Y2K   You're too kind

YA   Your

YAA   Yet another acronym

YABA   Yet another bloody acronym

YARLY   Ya, really?

YAS   Meaning "praise"

YBIC   Your brother in Christ

YBS   You'll be sorry

YCDBWYCID You can't do business when your computer is down

YCHT   You can have them

YCLIU   You can look it up

YCMU   You crack me up

YCT   Meaning Your comment to?

YD   Yesterday

YEET   Meaning excitement, approval or display of energy (i.e. throwing something)

YF   Wife

YG   Young gentleman

YGG   You go girl

YGTBKM   You've got to be kidding me

YGTR   You got that right

YHBT   You have been trolled

YHBW   You have been warned

YHL   You have lost

YIU   Yes, I understand

YKW   You know what

YKWYCD   You know what you can do

YL   Young lady

YMMV   Your mileage may vary

YNK   You never know

YOLO   You only live once

YR   Your

YR   Yeah right

YRYOCC You're running your own cuckoo clock

YSIC   Your sister in Christ

YSYD   Yeah sure you do

YT   YouTube

YT   You there?

YTB   You're the best

YTB   Youth talk back

YTTL   You take too long

YTG   You're the greatest

YW   You're welcome

YWHNB Yes, we have no bananas

YWHOL Yelling "woohoo" out loud

YWSYLS You win some, you lose some

YYSSW   Yeah, yeah, sure, sure, whatever

Z	Zero
Z	Z's are calling (meaning going to bed/sleep)
Z	Meaning "Said"
Z%	Zoo
ZH	Sleeping Hour
ZOMG	Used in World of Warcraft to mean OMG (Oh My God)
ZOT	Zero tolerance
ZUP	Meaning "What's up?"
ZZZZ	Sleeping (or bored)

Made in the USA
Monee, IL
10 December 2021

84573358R00056